NATION
GEOGRA
Ki

T0337312

PUZZLE BOOK

COOLEST

ANIMALS

Published by Collins
An imprint of HarperCollins Publishers
Westerhill Road
Bishopbriggs
Glasgow G64 2QT
www.harpercollins.co.uk

HarperCollins Publishers
1st Floor, Watermarque Building, Ringsend Road, Dublin 4, Ireland

In association with National Geographic Partners, LLC

NATIONAL GEOGRAPHIC and the Yellow Border Design are trademarks of the
National Geographic Society, used under license.

First published 2021

ISBN 978-0-00-843050-4

10 9 8 7 6 5 4 3 2

A catalogue record for this book is available from the British Library.

Printed in the UK

If you would like to comment on any aspect of this book,
please contact us at the above address or online.
natgeokidsbooks.co.uk
collins.reference@harpercollins.co.uk

Paper from responsible sources.

Acknowledgements

Cover images ©Shutterstock.com

P41 Superb bird of paradise © National Geographic Image Collection / Alamy
Stock Photo

All other images © Shutterstock.com

NATIONAL GEOGRAPHIC
KiDS

PUZZLE BOOK

COOLEST

ANIMALS

FACT-PACKED FUN

CONTENTS

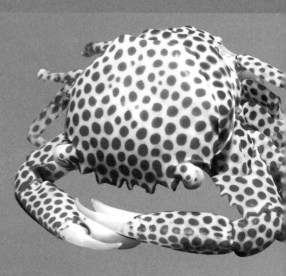

SPOTS AND STRIPES 6

COOL COLOURS 24

SUPER-FAST 42

CAMOUFLAGE 58

BIGGEST BEASTS 76

SOLUTIONS 94

SPOTS AND STRIPES

Let's get started with some puzzles and facts about awesome animals with striking spots and spectacular stripes!

BONGOS are a type of antelope that live in Africa. They have a brown coat with white stripes that makes for great camouflage in their forest habitat.

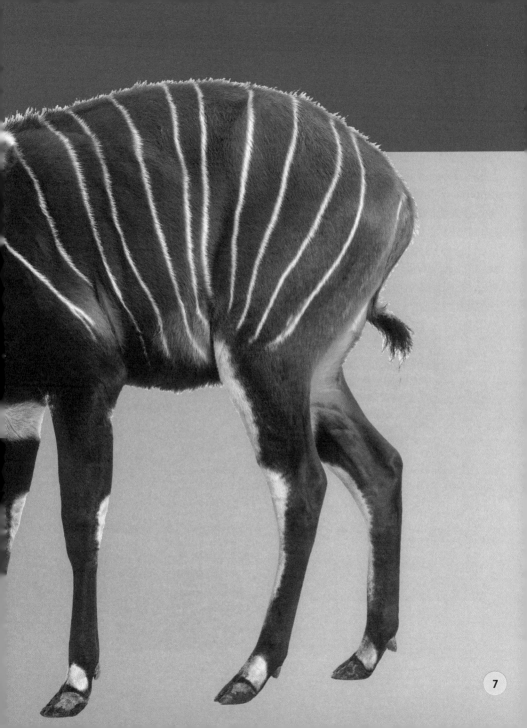

Crosswords

Help the tapir crack the crosswords by solving the clues below. Answers have the same amount of letters as the number in brackets. Can you work out the name of the spotted or striped creatures using the letters in the shaded squares? See if you are right by flicking to page 94.

BRAZILIAN TAPIRS are excellent swimmers and are closely related to rhinoceros!

Across
1 Move around in a circle (6)
6 Ship that goes underwater (9)
7 A desire or impulse (4)
8 The bill of a bird (4)
9 Lizard that can change colour (9)
11 Planet (6)

Down
1 Useful asset such as oil (8)
2 Sledge (8)
3 Hot drink (3)
4 The number 19 (8)
5 Saturdays and Sundays collectively (8)
10 You hear with this (3)

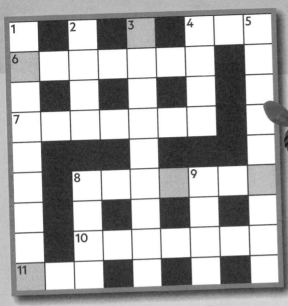

Across

4 Shade of a colour (3)
6 Include someone in an activity (7)
7 Pardon; excuse (7)
8 Segment of a book (7)
10 Loving dearly (7)
11 Container (3)

BLUE-BANDED BEES, unlike regular bees, live solitary lives and build burrows just under the soil.

Down

1 Not the same (9)
2 Finished (4)
3 Large reptile similar to a crocodile (9)
4 Where you are right now (4)
5 Urge on (9)
8 Marine crustacean that has pincers (4)
9 Stumble (4)

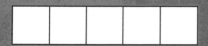

Sudokus

Help the mahi mahi solve the sudokus. Fill in the blank squares so that numbers 1 to 6 appear once in each row, column and 3 x 2 box. See if you are right by flicking to page 94.

MAHI MAHI are fast growing fish that can grow to 80 cm in length in less than six months.

4		3		2	
	4	6	3		
		5	4	6	
	1		2		5

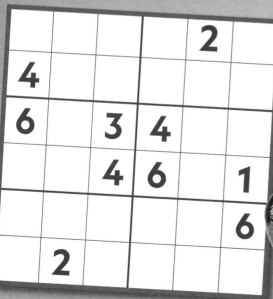

CORAL SNAKES are highly venomous. If they are under threat, coral snakes curl their tail so it looks like their head, which confuses attackers.

Wordsearches

The mimic octopus is on the hunt for other spotted and striped creatures. Can you help? Search left to right, up and down to find the words listed in the boxes below. See if you are right by flicking to page 94.

MIMIC OCTOPUSES change their markings and colour depending on what they are mimicking. They can impersonate anything from a flatfish to a snake.

bongo
bumblebee
lemur
numbat
okapi
skunk
tiger
zebra

a	y	l	s	d	u	i	i	i	o	p	x
j	g	e	e	e	a	u	t	o	t	u	r
w	s	l	e	m	u	r	t	k	z	u	b
m	r	s	e	n	u	m	b	a	t	j	u
u	b	w	z	h	e	k	i	p	p	x	m
h	u	e	z	v	e	a	l	i	b	n	b
t	u	k	e	o	x	i	h	a	o	a	l
i	g	s	b	a	r	s	s	t	n	l	e
g	n	s	r	e	v	b	k	t	g	b	b
e	j	o	a	p	h	k	u	u	o	n	e
r	q	t	u	a	u	d	n	r	t	i	e
r	p	t	h	u	q	b	k	b	a	e	t

b	c	l	a	d	y	b	i	r	d	f	r
l	t	y	t	m	i	d	d	b	y	i	e
s	c	h	x	i	e	a	p	b	z	s	o
m	h	t	e	e	h	l	u	s	l	w	r
g	i	z	b	p	x	m	l	e	l	m	p
f	t	a	g	i	r	a	f	f	e	g	r
e	a	a	e	u	s	t	m	z	o	l	q
k	l	v	p	m	t	i	f	f	p	t	i
i	h	y	e	n	a	a	c	o	a	p	i
g	h	f	t	s	i	n	k	a	r	a	g
a	w	s	a	l	a	m	a	n	d	e	r
p	j	a	g	u	a	r	c	a	l	p	t

chital	jaguar
dalmatian	ladybird
giraffe	leopard
hyena	salamander

PUFFERFISH have more than 100 species. They are also known by many other fun names like balloon fish, blowfish, globefish, toadfish and puffers!

13

Mazes

Scuttle like a crab around the maze until you reach the exit. See if you are right by flicking to page 95.

SEA SLUGS are related to snails. However, these creatures lost their shells as they have evolved.

Spot the difference

Compare the coral snake images below.
Can you spot the five differences between the images?
See if you are right by flicking to page 95.

Guess what?

1. **How many toes do Brazilian tapirs have?**
   a. Four on each foot
   b. Four on their front feet, three on their back feet
   c. Five on their front feet, three on their back feet

2. **What allows mimic octopuses to change their shape?**
   a. Lack of a rigid skeleton
   b. By sucking in water
   c. Eating a special fish

3. **What colour is a zebra's skin?**
   a. Black
   b. White
   c. Brown

4. **How far can a skunk spray?**
   a. 2 m
   b. 5 m
   c. 10 m

5. **What are red-spotted coral crabs also known as?**
   a. Police crabs
   b. Army crabs
   c. Guard crabs

6. **Where do blue-backed bees live?**
   a. Bee hives
   b. Inside trees
   c. Underground burrows

7. **What animal is the only living relative of the giraffe?**
   a. Okapi
   b. Elephant
   c. Llama

8. **'A _____ never changes its spots.' What animal is missing from this saying?**
   a. Hyena
   b. Dalmatian
   c. Leopard

9. **What is a group of tigers called?**
   a. A streak
   b. A pride
   c. A troop

10. **Coral snakes can reach an average length of?**
    a. 1 m
    b. 2 m
    c. 4 m

STRIPED HYENAS are the smallest species of hyena. They have been known to play dead to get out of sticky situations!

Can you guess the answers to the spotted and striped animal questions?
Check your answers by flicking to page 95.

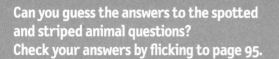

STRIPED MARLINS are some of the fastest fish in the sea. They use their speed, as well as their long bills, to stun their prey.

Close-ups

Animals with stripes come in all kinds of styles. Can you match these stripey creature close-ups on the left with the pictures below? See if you are right by flicking to page 95.

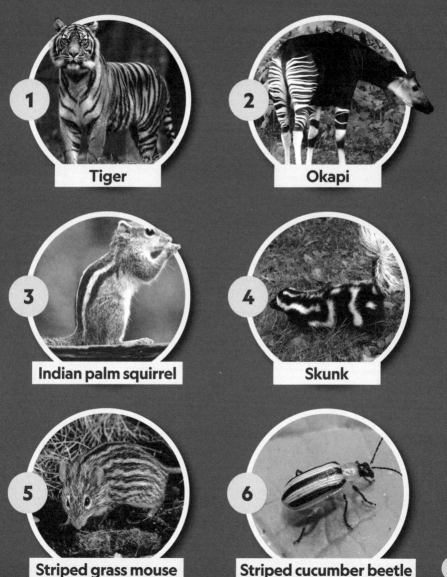

1 Tiger

2 Okapi

3 Indian palm squirrel

4 Skunk

5 Striped grass mouse

6 Striped cucumber beetle

Word jumbles

Rearrange the jumbled letters to form the names of five spotty or stripey species. See if you are right by flicking to page 95.

M E B B L U E B E

N S U K K

ZEBRAS are known for their stripes, but in some rare cases zebra foals can be born with spots!

WHALE SHARKS have completely unique patterns of stripes and spots on their skin that can be used as identification for each individual shark!

E R D A L P O

F O S W L I C N H

D O S T E P T

R T E T U L

COOL COLOURS

Get ready for some flashy facts and brilliant puzzles all about the most colourful of creatures!

BLUE DRAGON SEA SLUGS may look spectacular but they are very dangerous. Their favourite food is Portuguese man o' war – they keep the stinging cells of all the prey they eat to arm themselves with second-hand stingers!

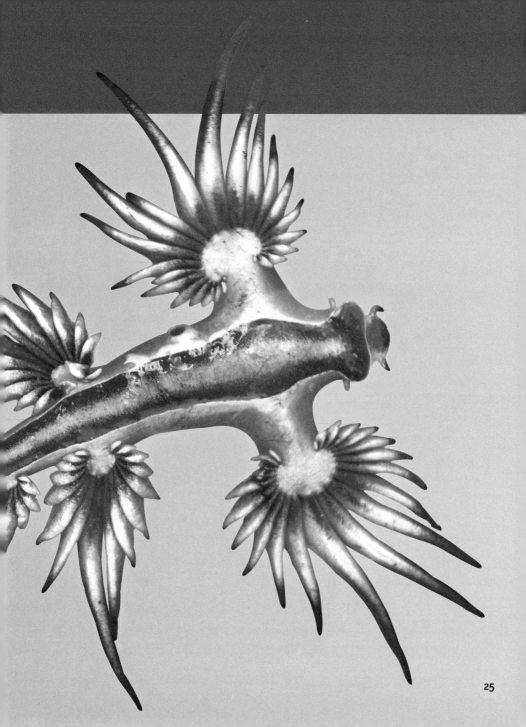

Crosswords

Help the sea star crack the crosswords by solving the clues below. Answers have the same amount of letters as the number in brackets. Can you work out the names of the cool-coloured creatures by using the letters in the shaded squares? See if you are right by flicking to page 96.

CROWN OF THORNS SEA STARS

can have up to 21 arms but most sea stars usually have five arms. Each of its arms are covered in venomous spines.

Across

4 Animal that looks like a tortoise (6)
6 Songbird (4)
7 Big cat that roars (4)
8 You often eat an ice cream from this (4)
9 Obtained (3)
10 Gentle shot on a golf course (4)
11 How tall a person is (6)

Down

1 Objects such as tables, chairs and desks (9)
2 Might; power (8)
3 Period of two weeks (9)
5 _____ guitar: type of musical instrument (8)

PINK DOLPHINS are dark grey at birth. They get their characteristic pink colouring when they mature.

Across

4 Say no to (6)
6 A word used to describe an action (4)
7 This grows on your head (4)
8 Big stone (4)
9 Someone you look up to (4)
10 60 seconds (6)

Down

1 Constant; lasting forever (9)
2 Fungus that is sometimes eaten as a vegetable (8)
3 Device used by people who jump out of aircraft (9)
5 All people (8)

(3, 4)

Sudokus

Help the bullfrog solve the sudokus. Fill in the blank squares so that numbers 1 to 6 appear once in each row, column and 3 x 2 box. See if you are right by flicking to page 96.

				2	3
	3				
		2	6	5	
	6	1	2		
				4	
4	1				

MALABAR GIANT SQUIRRELS are double the size of average grey squirrels and are a lot more colourful too! Instead of burying their food in the ground, this kind of squirrel is the only one known to hide future meals in the trees!

Wordsearches

blue
green
orange
pink
purple
red
turquoise
yellow

o	n	e	j	r	r	e	l	z	r	y	s
r	a	b	a	q	a	o	j	e	e	e	r
a	r	l	o	p	o	s	p	c	d	l	j
n	k	u	l	y	r	a	i	s	q	l	o
g	k	e	n	m	h	s	n	x	m	o	b
e	p	d	p	l	a	r	k	v	s	w	s
u	e	r	t	x	n	t	y	a	h	w	t
g	p	u	r	p	l	e	r	p	m	j	g
e	c	c	i	r	g	r	e	e	n	y	n
r	k	s	u	j	r	i	i	o	h	u	t
p	a	a	r	x	s	q	i	v	t	h	l
p	t	u	r	q	u	o	i	s	e	o	a

The pink katydid is on the lookout for colours and colourful creatures. Can you help? Search left to right, up and down to find the words listed in the boxes below. See if you are right by flicking to page 96.

p	e	a	c	o	c	k	r	b	g	l	w
p	t	s	h	f	w	r	z	l	m	p	r
t	p	j	a	h	w	a	b	u	a	s	r
j	s	a	m	r	b	i	r	e	n	i	v
a	z	t	e	c	b	l	i	j	d	a	p
u	x	e	l	g	i	p	l	a	r	e	a
s	w	o	e	m	b	e	y	y	i	t	e
r	t	u	o	f	j	t	m	p	l	m	t
r	t	p	n	s	v	m	v	l	l	f	c
a	e	z	n	f	l	a	m	i	n	g	o
d	r	g	o	n	x	p	m	a	c	a	w
t	r	e	e	f	r	o	g	s	e	g	t

blue jay
chameleon
flamingo
macaw
mandrill
peacock
tree frog

PINK KATYDID BUSH CRICKETS are extremely rare. One theory is that their pink colouring means they are more likely to be eaten by predators!

31

Mazes

Fly around the maze until you reach the exit.
See if you are right by flicking to page 97.

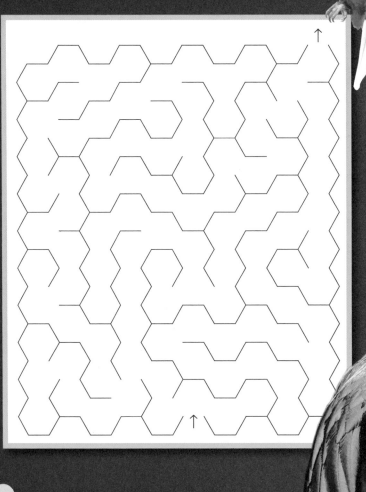

QUETZALS were once worshipped by the Aztec people because of their magnificent tail feathers that can grow up to 60 cm long!

PURPLE SEA SNAILS create their own raft of bubbles. They use the raft to float around near the surface of the ocean!

Spot the difference

Compare the scarlet macaw images below.
Can you spot the five differences between the images?

See if you are right by flicking to page 97.

Guess what?

1. What percentage of a peacock's whole length is made up by its beautiful tail?
   a. 15%
   b. 30%
   c. 60%

2. Where can you find rainbow grasshoppers' ears?
   a. On their head
   b. On their abdomen
   c. On their back

3. What do male Siamese fighting fish build nests out of?
   a. Bubbles
   b. Leaves
   c. Seaweed

4. What colour are pink dolphins when they are born?
   a. Dark pink
   b. Dark green
   c. Dark grey

5. How many species of macaws are there?
   a. 7
   b. 17
   c. 27

6. Which Amazonian bird has a colourful beak?
   a. Hummingbird
   b. Toucan
   c. Stork

7. Purple sea snails are also known as?
   a. Bubble raft snails
   b. Tinky winky snails
   c. Violet float snail

8. How long can malabar giant squirrels grow?
   a. 5 m
   b. 3 m
   c. 1 m

9. Crown of thorns sea stars are colourful to show other animals they are?
   a. Attractive
   b. Venomous
   c. Friendly

10. What is the world's most colourful duck?
    a. Mallard
    b. Golden eye
    c. Mandarin

SIAMESE FIGHTING FISH get their striking colours as a result of years of selective breeding.

36

Can you guess the answers to the
colourful creature questions?
Check your answers by flicking to page 97.

RAINBOW GRASSHOPPERS' ears
are on their abdomens!
Many people think that crickets
make their chirping sound by
rubbing their legs together,
however, the noise actually comes
from rubbing pegs on their
hind legs against their wings.

Close-ups

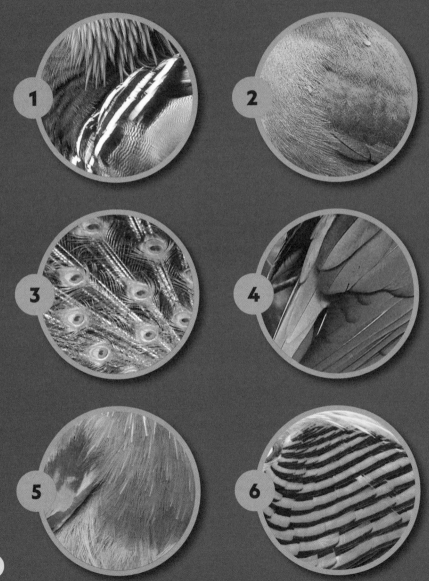

Birds often have breathtakingly brilliant feathers. Can you match these colourful bird close-ups on the left with the pictures below? See if you are right by flicking to page 97.

1 Peacock

2 Scarlet macaw

3 Motmot

4 Lilac-breasted roller

5 Mandarin duck

6 Golden pheasant

Word jumbles

Rearrange the jumbled letters to form the names of five colourful creatures. See if you are right by flicking to page 97.

L B E U   T R A D

G R F O

E R D   A D A N P

TEMMINCK'S TRAGOPAN is considered to be one of the most beautiful pheasants in the world. The males of its kind have a brilliant blue and scarlet bib that is used as part of a dance to impress females.

SUPERB BIRD OF PARADISE has special structures in its black feathers that make them absorb more light than usual. This means that they look almost impossibly black, which makes its turquoise plumage look even flashier!

M S A I T N

P R I M S H

A L O C R   K E S A N

H A L C A N E O M E

SUPER-FAST

Get ready to set some speed records with these fast facts and puzzles about some super speedy animals!

GIBBONS are amongt the world's fastest swinging animals. Their strong hands and long arms help them swing from branch to branch at over 50 km/h!

Crosswords

Help the cheetah crack the crosswords by solving the clues below. Answers have the same amount of letters as the number in brackets. Can you work out the names of the super-fast creatures by using the letters in the shaded squares? See if you are right by flicking to page 98.

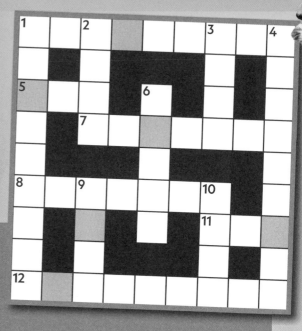

Across
1   The night of 31 October (9)
5   Mat (3)
7   E.g. biology or chemistry (7)
8   Things you wear (7)
11 Small green vegetable (3)
12 Crisis (9)

Down
1   Storm with a very strong wind (9)
2   Limbs used for walking (4)
3   Flat or level (4)
4   Obligatory or required (9)
6   The ability to see (5)
9   A single time (4)
10 Turn around quickly (4)

ELEPHANT SHREWS are one of the fastest small mammals. This short-legged, pointy-snouted sprinter can run at 28 km/h.

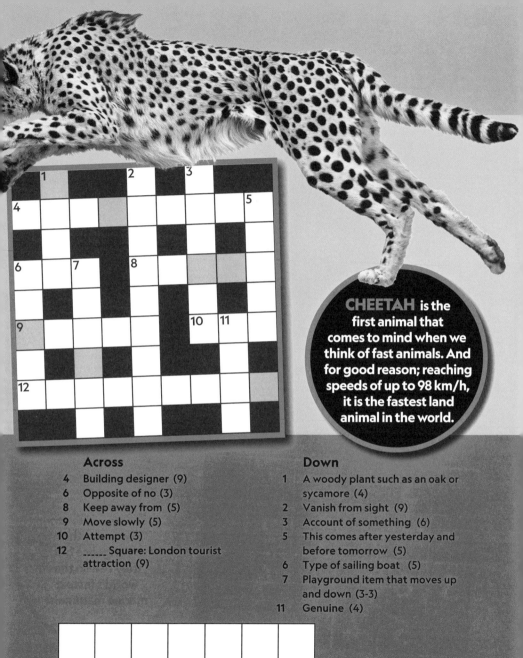

CHEETAH is the first animal that comes to mind when we think of fast animals. And for good reason; reaching speeds of up to 98 km/h, it is the fastest land animal in the world.

Across

4 Building designer (9)
6 Opposite of no (3)
8 Keep away from (5)
9 Move slowly (5)
10 Attempt (3)
12 _____ Square: London tourist attraction (9)

Down

1 A woody plant such as an oak or sycamore (4)
2 Vanish from sight (9)
3 Account of something (6)
5 This comes after yesterday and before tomorrow (5)
6 Type of sailing boat (5)
7 Playground item that moves up and down (3-3)
11 Genuine (4)

Sudokus

Help the dolphins solve the sudokus. Fill in the blank squares so that numbers 1 to 6 appear once in each row, column and 3 x 2 box. See if you are right by flicking to page 98.

5			2	6	
	2			1	4
	3				
				2	
3	6			4	
	5	4			2

DOLPHINS are known for their intelligence but they're also the world's fastest marine mammals.

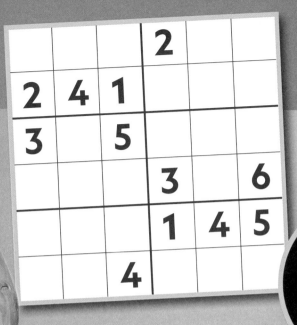

Wordsearches

This horsefly is on the hunt for other super-fast creatures. Can you help? Search left to right, up and down to find the words listed in the boxes below. See if you are right by flicking to page 98.

- albatross
- bats
- eagle
- falcon
- frigatebird
- horse fly
- hummingbird
- swift

t	f	r	i	g	a	t	e	b	i	r	d
j	m	a	r	h	p	e	h	s	v	e	h
t	j	s	a	o	d	t	u	j	z	a	b
i	h	w	s	r	a	m	m	k	b	g	p
y	g	i	o	s	l	j	m	y	r	l	w
r	s	f	a	e	b	y	i	g	w	e	f
n	p	t	l	f	a	f	n	x	o	r	q
b	m	p	e	l	t	x	g	b	a	t	s
w	g	p	u	y	r	l	b	k	l	t	u
r	f	a	l	c	o	n	i	j	t	i	j
u	f	q	s	d	s	d	r	s	q	u	x
g	e	l	t	h	s	f	d	r	r	u	s

HORSEFLIES could be the fastest flying insects, with an estimated speed of 145 km/h!

MEXICAN FREE-TAILED BATS are sometimes overlooked, but they're the fastest flying mammals on the planet! Their top horizontal flying speed is 99 km/h!

cheetah
dolphin
lion
marlin
pronghorn
sailfish
springbok
swordfish

a	p	r	o	n	g	h	o	r	n	l	u
k	v	s	a	u	n	o	i	t	j	j	e
c	s	w	o	r	d	f	i	s	h	a	z
h	t	l	d	x	x	a	i	l	s	s	j
e	s	i	s	w	k	s	i	h	p	l
e	d	o	l	p	h	i	n	m	r	r	r
t	e	n	s	h	h	t	s	a	a	i	m
a	v	u	i	b	a	i	e	r	f	n	d
h	r	p	j	j	t	l	r	l	f	g	p
s	a	i	l	f	i	s	h	i	s	b	e
l	k	b	t	k	o	u	s	n	s	o	p
e	j	i	l	t	a	a	t	s	f	k	w

Mazes

OSTRICHES are the fastest land birds. Reaching speeds of 70 km/h; they are a force to be reckoned with. They can run great distances because they have springy tendons in their legs that make running effortless.

Speed like a frigatebird around the maze
until you reach the exit. See if you are right
by flicking to page 99.

See if you are right by flicking to page 99.

FRIGATEBIRDS
can reach speeds of
over 140 km/h. Not only
fast, they have the
largest wing-area to
body-weight ratio of
any bird.

Spot the difference

Compare the skipper butterfly images below.
Can you spot the five differences between the images?
See if you are right by flicking to page 99.

Guess what?

1. A cheetah can go from 0 to 95 km/h in under?
   a. 3 seconds
   b. 3 minutes
   c. 30 minutes

2. What is the fastest fish in the ocean?
   a. Blue shark
   b. Bluefin tuna
   c. Sailfish

3. What are a group of dolphins called?
   a. A school
   b. A pod
   c. A herd

4. How fast do Australian tiger beetles run?
   a. 1 km/h
   b. 9 km/h
   c. 20 km/h

5. What is the fastest animal in the world?
   a. Shire horse
   b. Bull shark
   c. Peregrine falcon

6. Where do ruby-throated hummingbirds migrate to in the winter?
   a. Mexico and Central America
   b. Africa
   c. South America

7. How fast can ostriches run?
   a. 40 km/h
   b. 70 km/h
   c. 100 km/h

8. What reptile runs the fastest?
   a. Black spiny-tailed lizard
   b. Black mamba
   c. Green iguana

9. How wide is the wingspan of frigatebirds?
   a. 60 cm
   b. 1.2 m
   c. 2.4 m

10. The Mexican free-tailed bat is the official flying mammal of which US state?
    a. New York
    b. California
    c. Texas

PEREGRINE FALCONS are the fastest animals on Earth. When diving from great heights, they can reach speeds of up to 390 km/h!

Can you guess the answers to the super fast animal questions? Check your answers by flicking to page 99.

MALE RUBY-THROATED HUMMINGBIRDS can beat their wings more than 50 times per second.

Word jumbles

Rearrange the jumbled letters to form the
names of five super-fast creatures.
See if you are right by flicking to page 99.

H E C T E A H

H O L D I N P

**WHITE-
THROATED
NEEDLETAILS**
are one of the world's
fastest birds. While the
birds are in flight, they
use their wide beak to
catch insects.

T C O S R H I

G R E P E N R I E
A C L O N F

S R O H E   L Y F

CAMOUFLAGE

See if you can uncover the answers to these camo-tastic puzzles about the sneakiest of animals!

CHAMELEONS are masters of camouflage. They don't just change colour to blend in with their surroundings, they also change colour to regulate their body temperature and to communicate with other chameleons.

Crosswords

Help the butterfly crack the crosswords by solving the clues below. Answers have the same amount of letters as the number in brackets. Can you work out the names of the camouflage creatures by using the letters in the shaded squares? See if you are right by flicking to page 100.

DEAD LEAF BUTTERFLIES fold up their wings so that they look like dead leaves!

Across

1 Birds of prey that hoot (4)
3 Secure (4)
5 Kit (9)
6 Opposite of cheap (9)
8 List of school lessons and when they happen (9)
10 Certain (4)
11 A large number; numerous (4)

Down

1 These are made from beaten eggs cooked in frying pans (9)
2 Give out a bright light (5)
3 E.g. 2 + 2 (3)
4 Very (9)
7 A large group of insects (5)
9 Organ you see with (3)

COMMON BARON CATERPILLARS have long feather-like strands that come out in all directions. The strands mirror the veins of leaves so that the caterpillars can stay undetected.

Across

4 Evoker (anag.) (6)
6 Before long (4)
7 Household animal (3)
8 Not hot (4)
9 Metallic element (4)
10 Goal or purpose (3)
11 South Asian garment (4)
12 Stinging plant (6)

Down

1 Not permanent (9)
2 Grumble; moan (8)
3 Reptile with sharp teeth (9)
5 Guess (8)

(5,6)

Sudokus

Help the sea dragon solve the sudokus. Fill in the blank squares so that numbers 1 to 6 appear once in each row, column and 3 x 2 box. See if you are right by flicking to page 100.

5				1	
			5		
3			1		5
2		5			6
		4			
	3				4

GLAUERT'S SEADRAGONS, also called leafy seadragons, look remarkably like seaweed!

		3			
			3	2	5
	3	1			2
6			5	3	
3	1	6			
			1		

1				4	
	4			2	
	6	1			
			3	1	
	2			3	
	1				4

DECORATOR CRABS camouflage themselves with algae and tiny sea anemones to help them blend into the rocks or the seafloor.

Wordsearches

This great horned owl is on the hunt for camouflage words and creatures. Can you help? Search left to right, up and down to find the words listed in the boxes below. See if you are right by flicking to page 100.

t	u	d	i	s	g	u	i	s	e	l	t
t	f	a	m	b	u	s	h	d	l	a	d
p	s	u	r	r	o	u	n	d	i	n	g
r	a	j	e	m	a	s	t	a	d	v	d
o	o	n	s	s	t	h	h	s	l	t	i
t	v	t	u	h	i	d	d	e	n	g	s
e	q	o	o	i	b	s	e	b	i	y	a
c	c	a	m	o	u	f	l	a	g	e	p
t	r	l	p	r	w	a	y	u	p	c	p
i	m	g	z	r	e	y	p	i	l	s	e
o	u	n	d	e	t	e	c	t	e	d	a
n	v	i	i	v	s	r	e	k	z	j	r

GREAT HORNED OWLS are excellently camouflaged among the trees thanks to their bark-like feathers.

ambush
camouflage
disappear
disguise
hidden
protection
surrounding
undetected

GREAT POTOOS are large and bizarre-looking birds, with an even weirder call – they sound just like they are shouting 'Mum!' in a husky voice!

n	s	e	a	d	r	a	g	o	n	j	g
s	e	p	z	q	p	i	h	r	s	y	s
t	e	q	a	t	y	k	a	g	m	v	o
i	u	c	h	a	m	e	l	e	o	n	b
c	a	m	o	j	e	x	f	c	v	a	u
k	f	r	a	l	b	v	m	k	k	u	t
i	g	t	r	r	a	x	g	o	q	o	t
n	s	t	o	n	e	f	i	s	h	j	e
s	c	a	t	e	r	p	i	l	l	a	r
e	j	g	b	a	u	g	j	n	z	f	f
c	c	y	a	m	p	o	t	o	o	x	l
t	a	u	e	r	r	c	p	p	v	p	y

butterfly
caterpillar
chameleon
gecko
potoo
seadragon
stick insect
stonefish

Mazes

Venture around the maze until you reach the exit. See if you are right by flicking to page 101.

LEAF-TAILED GECKOS have tails that look just like leaves! The rest of their bodies look like leaves too.

REEF STONEFISH are venomous fish that can blend perfectly into their coral reef surroundings. They usually sit completely still until it is is time to ambush their prey!

Spot the difference

Compare the chameleon images below.
Can you spot the five differences between the images?
See if you are right by flicking to page 101.

Guess what?

1. Which master of camouflage has a super-fast tongue?
   a. Chameleons
   b. Great potoos
   c. Stick insects

2. What colour is cuttlefish blood?
   a. Red-orange
   b. Blue-green
   c. Yellow-green

3. What do stick insect eggs look like?
   a. Seeds
   b. Rice
   c. Beans

4. Leaf-tailed geckos do not have any?
   a. Toes
   b. Teeth
   c. Eyelids

5. Decorator crabs use what to camouflage themselves?
   a. Algae and sea anemones
   b. Sticks
   c. Leaves

6. Which shark's name means 'shaggy beard'?
   a. Carpet shark
   b. Wobbegong shark
   c. Thresher shark

7. Which family member does a great potoos call sound like?
   a. Dad
   b. Aunt
   c. Mum

8. The tail of a male leafy seadragon turns which colour when he is ready to mate?
   a. Yellow
   b. Red
   c. Purple

9. How do dead leaf butterflies make themselves look like leaves?
   a. Fold up their wings
   b. Lie on their back
   c. Flutter their wings

10. Why might an animal use camouflage?
    a. To attract mates
    b. To hide from predators
    c. To increase speed

STICK INSECTS, also known as walking sticks, are the longest insects in the world. These camouflage experts have limbs that look like twigs, even complete with fake buds!

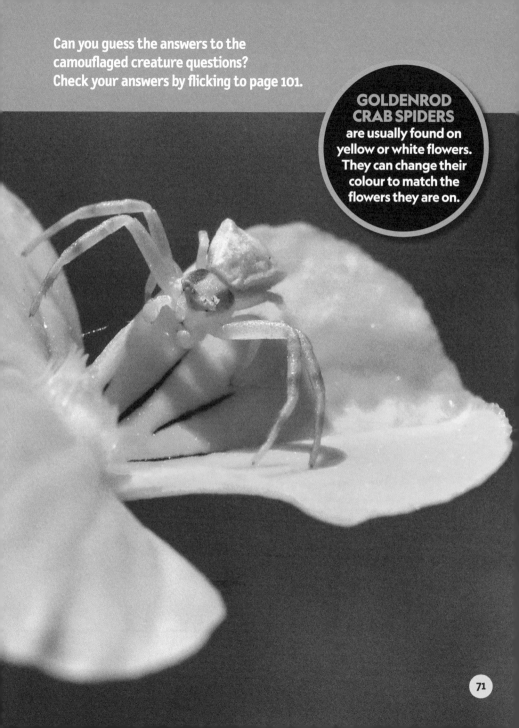

Can you guess the answers to the
camouflaged creature questions?
Check your answers by flicking to page 101.

**GOLDENROD
CRAB SPIDERS**
are usually found on
yellow or white flowers.
They can change their
colour to match the
flowers they are on.

Word jumbles

Rearrange the jumbled letters to form
the names of five masters of camouflage.
See if you are right by flicking to page 101.

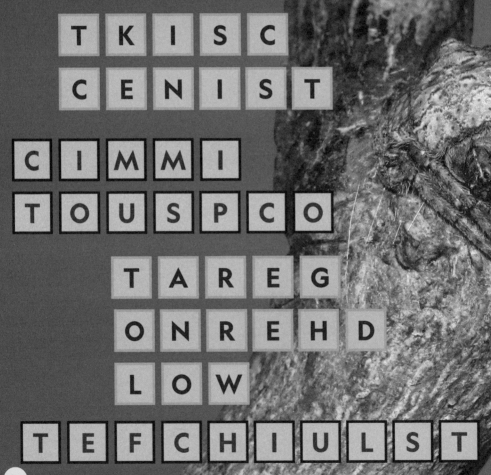

T K I S C
C E N I S T

C I M M I
T O U S P C O

T A R E G
O N R E H D
L O W

T E F C H I U L S T

WRAP-AROUND SPIDERS wrap their bodies all the way around branches and blend in with the bark. This helps the spiders hide from predators.

WOBBEGONG SHARKS get their name from an Aborigine word meaning 'shaggy beard'. The frills all around their heads look like beards and help the sharks to blend into the sea bed and ambush prey.

Word wheels

Can you spell a camouflaged creature using all of the letters in each word wheel? See if you are right by flicking to page 101.

VIETNAMESE MOSSY FROGS have evolved astonishingly real-looking 'moss' around the edge of their bodies so they can blend in and go unnoticed by predators.

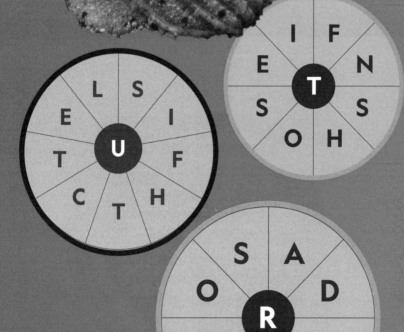

BIGGEST BEASTS

It's time to be seriously impressed by gigantic facts and some super-sized puzzles all about the largest animals on our planet!

AFRICAN BUSH ELEPHANTS are the largest land animals in the world. Males weigh an average of 5,500 kg – that's the weight of around 90 humans!

Crosswords

Help the tortoise crack the crosswords by solving the clues below. Answers have the same amount of letters as the number in brackets. Can you work out the names of the big beasts using the letters in the shaded squares? See if you are right by flicking to page 102.

Across

1 Material (9)
5 Large fruit (9)
8 Once more (5)
9 Amuse (9)
12 Tips over (9)

Down

1 Batman or Wonder Woman, for example (9)
2 Where you put rubbish (3)
3 Sleep during the day (3)
4 Big animals with ivory tusks (9)
6 Impressive bird of prey (5)
7 Write words without joining letters together (5)
10 A body part connected to your foot (3)
11 Port in Scotland; ray (anag.) (3)

TREE WETA are the heaviest insects around. They can weigh 70 g (around the same as a large egg)!

GIANT TORTOISES can live for over 100 years. They are the largest tortoises and can measure over 1.5 metres in length.

Across

1 Describe; make clear (7)
5 Belonging to us (3)
6 Where horses are kept (7)
8 Monarch; head of state (5)
9 Popular ice cream flavour (7)
11 Wonder or amazement (3)
12 Person who looks after teeth (7)

Down

1 Absolutely necessary (9)
2 The whole of (3)
3 Part of the nose (7)
4 Very good (9)
7 Reached a destination (7)
10 Member of a religious community of women (3)

(4,4)

Sudokus

Help the blue whale solve the sudokus.
Fill in the blank squares so that numbers 1 to 6
appear once in each row, column and 3 x 2 box.
See if you are right by
flicking to page 102.

BLUE WHALES are
the biggest animals ever
to exist. They weigh an
astonishing 150,000 kg and
can be as long as 30 m.
That's about the length of
three double-decker
buses in a row!

			6	3		
		2			6
3	2		1		
	1			2	3
5			2		
		4	6		

WANDERING ALBATROSSES have the largest wingspan in the animal kingdom, measuring almost 3.5 m wide!

Wordsearches

This Chinese salamander is on the hunt for other big beasts. Can you help? Search left to right, up and down to find the words listed in the boxes below. See if you are right by flicking to page 102.

CHINESE GIANT SALAMANDERS are the largest amphibians on the planet. They can grow up to 1.8 m long and weigh up to 50 kg!

blue whale
brown bear
capybara
elephant
giraffe
hippopotamus
salamander
squid

c	s	q	u	i	d	g	x	s	p	i	l
a	a	r	e	l	e	p	h	a	n	t	k
c	a	p	y	b	a	r	a	l	s	t	u
w	z	h	h	n	k	b	u	a	r	b	d
p	g	j	k	l	r	r	u	m	m	l	h
h	i	p	p	o	p	o	t	a	m	u	s
c	r	t	s	r	n	w	w	n	g	e	f
h	a	s	t	d	h	n	a	d	e	w	g
b	f	y	s	t	d	b	l	e	t	h	t
n	f	l	h	o	e	e	i	r	s	a	t
q	e	a	i	v	b	a	n	j	d	l	b
b	g	p	a	t	s	r	k	e	e	e	t

```
w q p o l a r b e a r f
t z s p e r m w h a l e
p v t e v h u m a a u r
p s a h a i r i c o j a
a n a c o n d a r s a l
i r r s w o o j o t v b
a r r t e c r m c r t a
v u p t l e n e o i a t
s k a z p r n z d c e r
s t r p e o p e i h o o
k o a o o s t l l w p s
s e a s t a r h e j s s
```

albatross
anaconda
crocodile
ostrich

polar bear
rhinoceros
sea star
sperm whale

ANTS have the largest population on land of any creature. It is estimated that there are ten billion billion!

Mazes

Strut around the maze until you
reach the exit. See if you are right
by flicking to page 103.

GIRAFFES are the
tallest animals in the
world, measuring in
at almost 6 m!

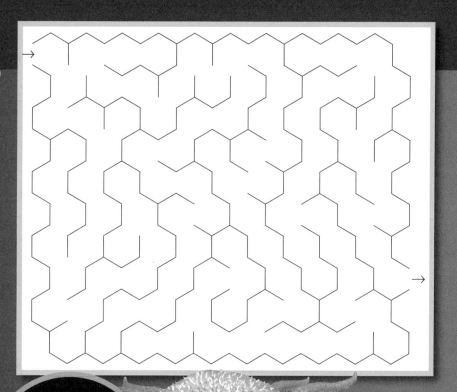

SUNFLOWER SEA STARS are the biggest sea stars in the world. These chunky beasts can weigh up to 5 kg, and have as many as 24 arms!

Spot the difference

Compare the elephant images below.
Can you spot the five differences between the images?
See if you are right by flicking to page 103.

Guess what?

1. **Wild African elephants can eat up to how much food a day?**
   a. 15 kg
   b. 75 kg
   c. 150 kg

2. **What is the biggest reptile in the world?**
   a. Saltwater crocodile
   b. Leatherback turtle
   c. Komodo dragon

3. **Giant tortoises can weigh up to?**
   a. 50 kg
   b. 125 kg
   c. 300 kg

4. **A colossal squid's eye can be as big as a:**
   a. Football
   b. Beach ball
   c. Tennis ball

5. **Sperm whales can grow to a maximum of?**
   a. 6 m
   b. 11 m
   c. 17 m

6. **How wide can a wandering albatrosses' wingspan be?**
   a. 1.5 m
   b. 2.5 m
   c. 3.5 m

7. **What does 'tree weta' mean in Maori language?**
   a. God of ugly things
   b. God of tall things
   c. God of smelly things

8. **How long is a giraffe's tongue?**
   a. 50 cm
   b. 30 cm
   c. 20 cm

9. **What is a blue whale's heart the same size as?**
   a. A bicycle
   b. A car
   c. A bus

10. **Which snake can grow up to 5 m long?**
    a. King cobra
    b. Rattle snake
    c. Green anaconda

SALTWATER CROCODILES are the heaviest reptiles on the planet and can weigh as much as 1,300 kg.

Can you guess the answers to the big beast questions?
Check your answers by flicking to page 103.

SPERM
WHALES have the
heaviest brains of
any animal.

Close-ups

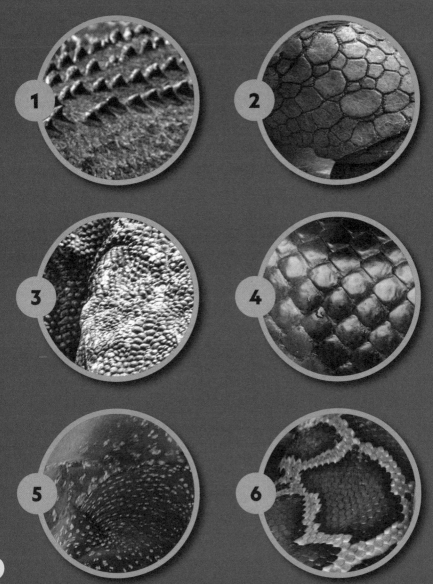

Can you match these close-ups of the enormous reptiles on the left with the pictures below? See if you are right by flicking to page 103.

1 Anaconda

2 Komodo dragon

3 Saltwater crocodile

4 Leatherback sea turtle

5 Python

6 Giant tortoise

Word jumbles

Rearrange the jumbled letters to form the names of five big animals. See if you are right by flicking to page 103.

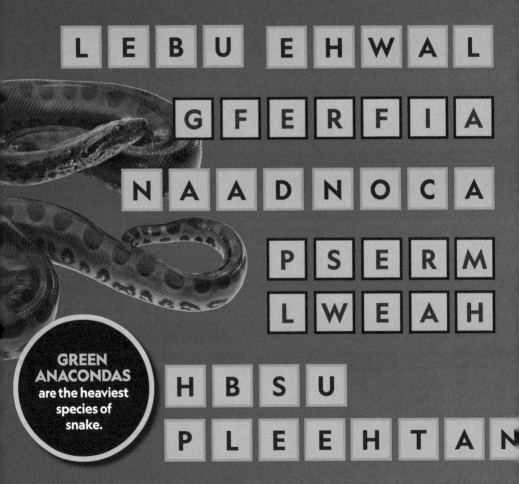

L E B U E H W A L

G F E R R F I A

N A A D N O C A

P S E R M
L W E A H

H B S U
P L E E H T A N

GREEN ANACONDAS are the heaviest species of snake.

POLAR BEARS are the largest carnivores on land. Despite their size, polar bears are fantastic swimmers!

SOLUTIONS

Pages 8-9

```
R O T A T E
R E O E N W
S U B M A R I N E
O O O N E
U R G E   B E A K
R G T E
C H A M E L E O N
E N A E D
U R A N U S
```
Keyword: BONGO

```
D O A   H U E
I N V O L V E N
F E L R C
F O R G I V E O
E G U
R C H A P T E R R
E R T R A
N A D O R I N G
T U B R P E
```
Keyword: TAPIR

Pages 10-11

2	6	1	5	4	3
4	5	3	1	2	6
1	4	6	3	5	2
3	2	5	4	6	1
6	1	4	2	3	5
5	3	2	6	1	4

5	6	2	1	3	4
3	1	4	5	2	6
4	3	1	2	6	5
6	2	5	4	1	3
2	5	6	3	4	1
1	4	3	6	5	2

5	6	1	3	2	4
4	3	2	1	6	5
6	1	3	4	5	2
2	5	4	6	3	1
3	4	5	2	1	6
1	2	6	5	4	3

Pages 12-13

```
a y l s d u i i i o p x
j g e e e a u t o t u r
w s l e m u r t k z u b
m r s e n u m b a t j u
u b w z h e k i p p x m
h u e z v e a l i b n b
t u k e o x i h a o a l
i g s b a r s s t n l e
g n s r e v b k t g b o
e j o a p h k u u o n e
r q t u a u d n r t i e
r p t h u q b k b e e t
```

```
b c l a d y b i r d f r
l t y t m i d d b y i e
s c h x i e a p b z s o
m h t e e h l u s l w r
g i z b p x m l e l m p
f t a g i r a f f e g r
e a a e u s t m z o l q
k l v p m t i f f p t i
i h y e n a a c o a p i
g h f t s i n k a r a g
a w s a l a m a n d e r
p j a g u a r c a l p t
```

94

Pages 14–15

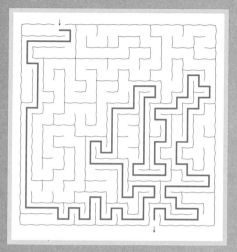

Pages 16–17

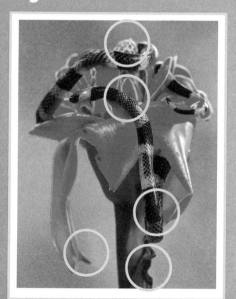

Page 18

1. b. Four on their front feet, three on their back feet
2. a. Lack of a rigid skeleton
3. a. Black
4. b. 5 m
5. c. Guard crabs
6. c. Underground burrows
7. a. Okapi
8. c. Leopard
9. a. A streak
10. b. 2 m

Pages 20–21

1 – 4 Skunk

2 – 6 Striped cucumber beetle

3 – 3 Indian palm squirrel

4 – 2 Okapi

5 – 5 Striped grass mouse

6 – 1 Tiger

Pages 22–23

Bumblebee
Skunk
Leopard
Clownfish
Spotted turtle

SOLUTIONS

Pages 26–27

Keyword: PEACOCK

Keyword: SEA STAR

Pages 28–29

1	5	6	4	2	3
2	3	4	5	1	6
3	4	2	6	5	1
5	6	1	2	3	4
6	2	3	1	4	5
4	1	5	3	6	2

5	3	2	6	4	1
4	6	1	2	3	5
3	5	6	4	1	2
2	1	4	5	6	3
6	2	3	1	5	4
1	4	5	3	2	6

6	4	3	2	1	5
2	5	1	3	4	6
4	2	5	1	6	3
1	3	6	4	5	2
5	1	2	6	3	4
3	6	4	5	2	1

Pages 30–31

Pages 32-33

Pages 34-35

Page 36

1. c. 60%
2. b. On their abdomen
3. a. Bubbles
4. c. Dark grey
5. b. 17
6. b. Toucan
7. a. Bubble raft snails
8. c. 1m
9. b. Venomous
10. c. Mandarin

Pages 38-39

1-5 Mandarin duck
2-3 Motmot
3-1 Peacock
4-2 Scarlet macaw
5-4 Lilac-breasted roller
6-6 Golden pheasant

Pages 40-41

Blue dart frog
Red panda
Mantis shrimp
Coral snake
Chameleon

SOLUTIONS

Pages 44–45

H	A	L	L	O	W	E	E	N
U		E		V				E
R	U	G		S	E	C		C
R		S	C	I	E	N	C	E
I			G			E		S
C	L	O	T	H	E	S		S
A		N		T		P	E	A
N		C		I				R
E	M	E	R	G	E	N	C	Y

Keyword: MARLIN

	T		D		R			
A	R	C	H	I	T	E	C	T
	E		S		P		O	
Y	E	S		A	V	O	I	D
A		E		P		R		A
C	R	E	E	P		T	R	Y
H		S		E			E	
T	R	A	F	A	L	G	A	R
	W		R		R		L	

Keyword: OSTRICH

Pages 46–47

5	4	1	2	6	3
6	2	3	5	1	4
2	3	6	4	5	1
4	1	5	3	2	6
3	6	2	1	4	5
1	5	4	6	3	2

5	3	6	2	1	4
2	4	1	5	6	3
3	6	5	4	2	1
4	1	2	3	5	6
6	2	3	1	4	5
1	5	4	6	3	2

1	3	2	4	5	6
5	4	6	2	3	1
4	2	1	5	6	3
3	6	5	1	2	4
2	1	3	6	4	5
6	5	4	3	1	2

Pages 48–49

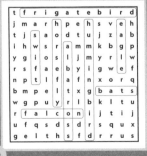

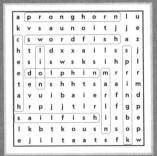

Pages 50–51

Pages 52–53

Page 54

1. a. 3 seconds
2. c. Sailfish
3. b. A pod
4. b. 9 km/h
5. c. Peregrine falcon
6. a. Mexico and Central America
7. b. 70 km/h
8. a. Black spiny-tailed lizard
9. c. 2.4 m
10. c. Texas

Pages 56–57

Cheetah
Dolphin
Ostrich
Peregrine falcon
Horsefly

SOLUTIONS

Pages 60-61

O	W	L	S		S	A	F	E
M			H		U			X
E	Q	U	I	P	M	E	N	T
L			N					R
E	X	P	E	N	S	I	V	E
T				W				M
T	I	M	E	T	A	B	L	E
E			Y		R			L
S	U	R	E		M	A	N	Y

Keyword: BUTTERFLY

	T		C			C		
R	E	V	O	K	E		R	
	M		M		S	O	O	N
	P		P	E	T		C	
C	O	O	L		I	R	O	N
	R		A	I	M		D	
S	A	R	I		A		I	
R	R		N	E	T	T	L	E
	Y				E		E	

Keyword: STICK INSECT

Pages 62-63

5	6	3	4	1	2
4	2	1	5	6	3
3	4	6	1	2	5
2	1	5	3	4	6
6	5	4	2	3	1
1	3	2	6	5	4

2	5	3	4	1	6
1	6	4	3	2	5
5	3	1	6	4	2
6	4	2	5	3	1
3	1	6	2	5	4
4	2	5	1	6	3

1	3	2	6	4	5
6	4	5	1	2	3
3	6	1	4	5	2
2	5	4	3	1	6
4	2	6	5	3	1
5	1	3	2	6	4

Pages 64-65

100

Pages 66-67

Pages 68-69

Page 70

1. a. Chameleons
2. b. Blue-green
3. a. Seeds
4. c. Eyelids
5. a. Algae and sea anemones
6. b. Wobbegong shark
7. c. Mum
8. a. Yellow
9. a. Fold up their wings
10. b. To hide from predators

Pages 72-73

Stick insect
Mimic octopus
Great horned owl
Cuttlefish

Page 75

Cuttlefish
Stonefish
Seadragon

SOLUTIONS

Pages 78-79

Keyword: CAPYBARA

Keyword: TREE WETA

Pages 80-81

4	5	6	3	1	2
1	3	2	4	5	6
3	2	5	1	6	4
6	4	1	5	2	3
5	6	3	2	4	1
2	1	4	6	3	5

6	3	4	1	2	5
2	5	1	3	4	6
1	2	6	4	5	3
3	4	5	2	6	1
5	1	2	6	3	4
4	6	3	5	1	2

6	5	2	3	4	1
4	3	1	2	6	5
2	6	4	1	5	3
5	1	3	4	2	6
1	2	6	5	3	4
3	4	5	6	1	2

Pages 82-83

Pages 84–85

Pages 86–87

Page 88

1. c. 150 kg
2. a. Saltwater crocodile
3. c. 300 kg
4. b. Beach ball
5. c. 17 m
6. c. 3.5 m
7. a. God of ugly things
8. a. 50 cm
9. b. A car
10. c. Green anaconda

Pages 90–91

1-3 Saltwater crocodile
2-6 Giant tortoise
3-2 Komodo dragon
4-1 Anaconda
5-4 Leatherback sea turtle
6-5 Python

Page 92

Blue whale
Giraffe
Anaconda
Sperm whale
Bush elephant

Look for more puzzle books in this series!